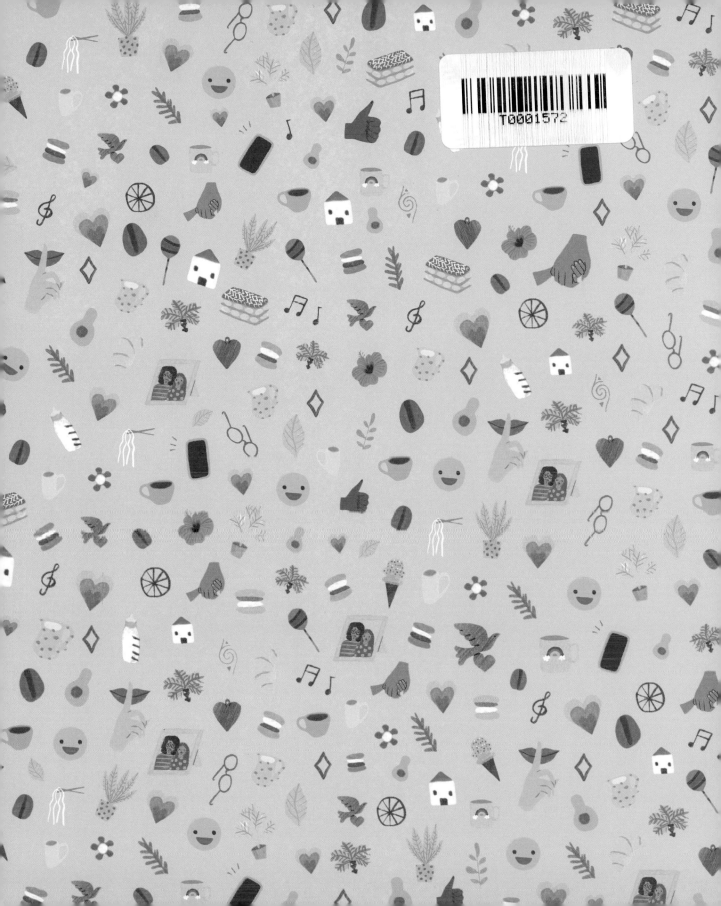

How to Greet a Grandma

WIDE EYED EDITIONS

There is no one quite like a grandma.

Grandmas can take on many roles:
teachers, playmates, heroes, life-coaches ...
They can be funny, wise, warm—and they
come with a variety of hairstyles!

Grandmas are found in every country in the
world. You might know yours as nanna, granny,
grams, memaw, gran-gran, or something else.
Every grandma is one of a kind, although
they often share some similarities.

In this book, you'll travel the world and visit different grandmas. You'll learn how to greet them and discover some of the traditions and wisdoms they might share with you.

Can you recognize any of these glorious global grandmas?

Let's celebrate every one of them!

What is a grandma?

A grandma isn't just a grandma,
she's a mom as well!

Her children had children,
giving her a special place
right at the top of the family.

You may have a grandma,
have had a grandma,
or have a few grandmas.

And it's very normal
to really like someone
else's grandma too.

Anatomy of a grandma

MIND
Full of clever solutions and funny memories of embarrassing things your parents once did.

EARS
Excellent for listening to all your best jokes.

MOUTH
Always ready with a smile and a story.

ARMS
Usually poised and available for hugs.

HANDS
Perfect for tickling, pinching cheeks, and rounds of applause.

HEART
Packed with a lifetime's worth of love.

FEET
At the ready for adventure, dancing, and setting a great example.

KNEES
Great for expertly bouncing grandbabies on.

Special grandma skills

Grandmas tend to be a little older than the rest of us, so it makes sense that they're so talented and wise—they've had a few extra years to figure things out!

There are some things that grandmas seem to do better than anyone else, do you recognize any of these amazing grandma skills?

Being the captain of the family, and steering them out of trouble

Masterminding excellent family activities

Weaving the best stories

Cheering on their
loved ones

Trying new
things and
learning new skills

Guiding
their families
through life

Pondering life's
big questions

Passing down
traditions

Grandma facts

You might think you already know quite a bit about grandmas,
but did you know ...

In France, the UK, and the US,
the average grandma has about
five grandchildren.

The average age
someone becomes a
grandma in the US is 50.

There is no
official world
record for
the grandma
with the most
grandchildren, but
some grandmas
have lived to
have over 100
grandchildren!

There are more
grandmothers in the
world than grandfathers.

Poland was the first country
to introduce a yearly
"Grandmother's Day"
celebration. It began in
1964 and Polish people have
celebrated their grandmas
on January 21st ever since.

Former US president Barack Obama was raised by his grandma and grandpa for many years.

Lots of women around the world still have jobs when they become grandmas.

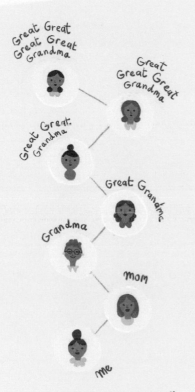

Great Great Great Great Grandma

Great Great Great Grandma

Great Great Grandma

Great Grandma

Grandma

mom

me

The most "greats" a grandma has been so far is a great-great-great-great grandma. That means seven generations alive in the same family!

Queen Elizabeth II of England is not only a queen, she's also a grandma, and great grandma.

Studies have found that spending quality time with grandchildren is good for grandparents' wellbeing—helping them stay happy and healthy!

Kon'nichiwa, Obaachan!

(oh-bah-chang)

More Japanese grandmas, or Obaachans, live to be over 100 years old than anywhere else in the world. All that life experience helps an Obaachan accumulate lots of helpful wisdom she can share. For instance, an Obaachan might show you how to wear traditional Japanese "geta"—special raised wooden sandals designed for walking in rain and snow—or she might tell you where to keep your towel when you bathe in an "onsen" (a Japanese hot spring)—folded neatly on your head, of course.

Noodles would be a good meal to share with an Obaachan. In Japan, people eat oodles of noodles and the best way to enjoy them is with a big slurp—an Obaachan won't mind!

WHERE TO SPOT AN OBAACHAN: *Japan*

HOW TO GREET HER: *Bow from the waist and say, "Kon'nichiwa"*

OBAACHAN WISDOM: *Fall seven times and stand up eight*

USEFUL PHRASE: *"Korera no men wa oishī desu."* (These noodles are delicious.)

Kia ora, Kuia!

(koo-yah)

The Māori are the indigenous people of New Zealand and a Māori grandma is called a Kuia. Tattoos are an important part of Māori culture and they often tell the story of a person's family history. Some Kuias have a special tattoo on their chin—this is called a "moko kauae."

An especially wise Kuia might teach you Māori traditions, such as the "kapa haka" group dance or she might share enchanting Māori myths and legends. Storytelling is a big part of Māori life, and most stories are memorized and spoken instead of written down in books—so, remember to listen when a Kuia starts to share!

Aloha, Tutu!

(too-too)

Tutu is what Hawaiian grandchildren call both their grandma and grandpa—nice and easy to remember. If you meet a Tutu, she's likely to be wearing a "muumuu," which is a loose-fitting Hawaiian dress, usually in a bright color and easy to dance in! If a Tutu invites you to a lūʻau (a Hawaiian party), you can expect lots of fun, food, and color. A Tutu will have been to so many lūʻaus, she'll know exactly how to throw a great one (and she'll be a pretty amazing guest, too)! She might even teach you how to "hula"—a traditional Hawaiian dance.

WHERE TO SPOT A TUTU: *Hawaii, US*

HOW TO GREET HER: *A kiss on the cheek and an "Aloha!"*

TUTU WISDOM: *Dare to dance, leave shame at home*

Hawaiians use the word "Ohana" to talk about their extended family, and this often includes people who aren't related to them, but who they love and care about. So, another person's Tutu can still be considered part of your family in Hawaii.

Selam, Sēti āyati!

(sey-tea-ah-tea)

An Ethiopian grandma, or Sēti āyati, is often a guardian of traditions who teaches younger generations treasured skills and lessons. One popular tradition she could teach you about is an Ethiopian coffee ceremony—a special way of preparing and serving coffee to family and friends. You could help a Sēti āyati by passing the filled coffee cups to her guests! Storytelling is another Ethiopian tradition, and a Sēti āyati will often share stories and pass down folktales as a way to teach her grandchildren important life lessons.

WHERE TO SPOT A SĒTI ĀYATI: *Ethiopia*

HOW TO GREET HER: *If you know her very well, three kisses on alternate cheeks*

SĒTI ĀYATI WISDOM: *Do not climb a ladder if you cannot yet walk*

Most Sēti āyatis will own a "gabi," this is a special cotton blanket that is usually white, with colored bands woven into it. A Sēti āyati will use this blanket for all kinds of useful things, including keeping her grandchildren warm!

Bonjour, Mémé!

(meh-meh)

What is a French Mémé's favorite day? Grandmother's Day, of course! Every year on the first Sunday in March, the French people celebrate and thank their Mémés for all that they do. If you want to give a Mémé a special gift on this day, an orchid plant is a popular present, and sure to make her smile.

A big part of French culture is food—especially the sweet stuff! And Mémés are often the ones passing down the cooking traditions. If you're feeling hungry, make sure to visit a Mémé at "L'heure de gouter," which is a late-afternoon snack time. The snack is often something chocolaty. Yum!

WHERE TO SPOT A MÉMÉ: *France*

HOW TO GREET HER: *Give her a kiss on each cheek and say, "Bonjour!"*

MÉMÉ WISDOM: *Little by little, the bird makes its nest*

USEFUL PHRASE: *"Merci, j'adore le chocolat!" (Thank you, I love chocolate!)*

Mémé's Gouter Treats

Chaussons Aux Pommes
Warm, apple-filled pastries. The French name means "apple slippers!"

Pain au chocolat
Layers of soft dough baked with pieces of chocolate inside.

Crêpes
Super thin pancakes. You can have sweet ones with sugar, fruits, or chocolate, or savory ones with ham, gooey cheese, and vegetables.

Madeleines
Simple, tasty sponge cakes baked in a shell shape.

Macarons
Colorful little round cakes made of meringue.

Mille-Feuille
A flaky treat made of thin sheets of pastry and filled with cream. The name "mille-feuille" means one thousand sheets, but these desserts are usually only made with three sheets of pastry.

Galette des rois
This delicious dessert's name means "King's cake," and it comes with a surprise! Baked into the buttery pastry is a tiny figurine—if you find it in your slice, your get to be king or queen for a day and wear a crown!

Ki kati, Bibi!

(bee-bee)

In Swahili (one of the languages of Uganda), a grandma is known as a "Bibi." You're likely to spot a Bibi outside in the garden. This is because most Ugandan women are expert farmers who grow their own fruits and vegetables, including matoke (a type of banana). A Bibi will use these homegrown crops to make delicious meals for her family. If a Bibi has cooked for you, make sure you've got a compliment ready, as it is tradition for each dinner guest to comment on the food!

WHERE TO SPOT A BIBI: Uganda

HOW TO GREET HER: Shake her hand and say, "Ki kati"

BIBI WISDOM: When the moon is not full, the stars shine more brightly

USEFUL PHRASE: "Asante, bibi!" (Thank you, grandma!)

On special occasions, Bibis often wear a beautiful colorful dress, known as a "gomesi" or a "busuuti," with a sash tied around the waist. Bibis from the west of Uganda might drape a long cloth called a "suuka" around their waists, too.

Kem cho, Nani / Ba!

(nan-nee / bah)

Do you have a different name for each of your grandmas? In India, people who speak the Gujarati language call their mom's mom Nani and their dad's mom Ba. No matter the name, it's common to see an Indian grandma wearing a "sari" (a long piece of beautiful fabric, folded in a special way) and "champal" slippers that make a flip-flop sound—so you can always hear her coming!

WHERE TO SPOT A NANI / BA: *India*

HOW TO GREET HER: Reach down and touch one of her feet, then touch your chest, over your heart as a mark of respect

NANI / BA WISDOM: If you dream for too long, you will become like your shadow

Nanis and Bas have lots of skills and knowledge to share. One might tell you all about henna—a dye that many Indian women have painted on their hands and feet for special occasions. Or she might show you how to use coconut oil to keep your hair shining like silk! On your birthday, she may give money as a gift, and it's lucky for the amount to end in 1.

Bonjou, Grann!

(gra-anne)

In Haiti, a Grann's job is often a bit like the boss of the family. She might help make decisions, set an example, and stay clued up on everyone's activities! Many Granns are also very social, often going to market with their friends and helping others at community events. Granns can also be fun-loving. Haiti is famous for its Easter celebrations, where people come together to play, listen, and dance to music—a Grann might join in by dancing or playing an instrument! Look out for her "karabela" dress—a beautiful dress in shades of red and blue, worn by many Haitian women on special occasions.

WHERE TO SPOT A GRANN: *Haiti*

HOW TO GREET HER: *A kiss on the cheek*

GRANN WISDOM: *Hope makes one live*

INSTRUMENTS A GRANN MIGHT PLAY

As well as bright costumes and dancing, Haitian festivals have lots of music! An especially musical Grann might play the accordion, guitar, or violin. For Granns who have a good sense of rhythm, any of the instruments below will do perfectly!

Vaksin
A cylindrical bamboo trumpet.

Maracas
A pair of rattles—perfect for those who like to dance while they shake!

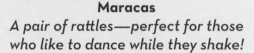

Empty cans and metal lids
Fantastic for Granns who like to upcycle and improvize!

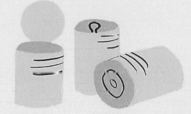

Drums
Can be beaten with hands or sticks. A tanbou is a type of Haitian barrel drum.

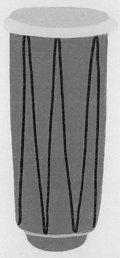

Güira
A metal cylinder pierced with holes—musicians scrape this instrument with a metal brush to produce a unique sound.

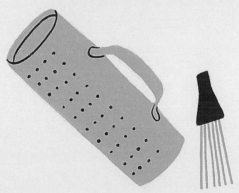

Privet, Babushka!

(ba-boosh-kah)

If you enjoy cozy comforts, a Russian grandma, called a Babushka, would be the perfect host. In a Babushka's home, it's polite to swap your shoes for snug slippers called "tapochki"—don't worry if you forget, as a Babushka will often have a spare pair to lend. As well as slippers, a Babushka may offer you a warm cup of tea followed by a good game of chess—both of which are very popular in Russia.

In many Russian families, Babushkas are in charge of special holidays—planning, cooking, and hosting—and a Babushka will often use these times to pass down traditions to her grandchildren.

WHERE TO SPOT A BABUSHKA: *Russia*

HOW TO GREET HER: *Shake her hand, look her in the eye, and say, "Privet"*

BABUSHKA WISDOM: *It's nice to visit, but it's better to be home*

USEFUL PHRASE: *"Mat!" (Checkmate!)*

Hola, Abuela!

(ab-weh-lah)

What three words best describe a Mexican grandma, or Abuela? Family, food, and fun! Abuelas are known as the heart and soul of their families. They often help raise their grandchildren and teach them all about Hispanic traditions. Getting together is super important for most Abuelas. To prepare for a big gathering, an Abuela might show you how to cook delicious tacos or craft "papel picado"—colorful decorative banners.

WHERE TO SPOT AN ABUELA: Mexico

HOW TO GREET HER: *A friendly "Hola," and a kiss on the cheek*

ABUELA WISDOM: *Full stomach, happy heart*

To thank their Abuelas—and abuelos (grandpas)—Mexicans celebrate Grandparent's Day on August 28th every year. The day is all about the bond between grandparents and their grandchildren, and it's another perfect reason for a party, of course!

Helo, Mamgu!

(mam-gee)

You might hear a Welsh grandma, or Mamgu, before you see her.
This is because in Wales—also known as the "Land of song"—music,
and singing especially, are a BIG part of life. Hymns are sung in churches,
at celebrations like weddings, and at sports events such as rugby matches,
and a Mamgu can teach you the best ones.

WHERE TO SPOT A MAMGU: South Wales, UK
(grandmas from North Wales are
called "Nain")

HOW TO GREET HER: With a "Helo" and a hug

MAMGU WISDOM: Speak well of your friend,
of your enemy say nothing

You might notice a special type of spoon in a Mamgu's house, this isn't something
she'd use for eating ice cream, though! It's usually quite big, carved out of wood, and
known as a "love spoon." In the past, love spoons were given as a way to win over
sweethearts and the carvings showed off the skills of the person who made it.

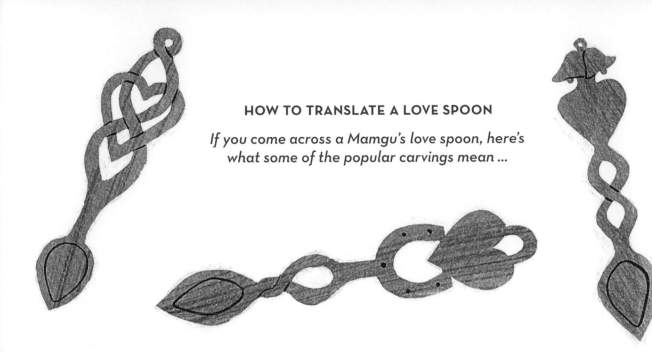

HOW TO TRANSLATE A LOVE SPOON

If you come across a Mamgu's love spoon, here's what some of the popular carvings mean ...

Dragon:
Protection

Anchor:
Settling down

Dove:
Peace

Heart:
Love

Knot:
Eternal love

Horseshoe:
Good luck

Diamond:
Wealth and good fortune

Key:
Home and security

Twisted stem:
Togetherness

Kumusta po, Lola!

(low-lah)

Would you like to see your grandma every day? If so, a Lola would be perfect, since Filipina grandmas often live with their grandchildren. Sharing a home with a Lola is a way for her family to thank and take care of her, and also means a Lola is around to help, play, and tuck her grandkids in at night!

When you chat to a Lola, make sure to end your sentences with the word "po"—this is a way to show respect to your elders. But that doesn't mean that Lolas are serious and stiff—in fact, the Philippines is one of the happiest countries in the world, and its Lolas are famed for their friendliness, too. Fiestas and celebrations are enjoyed throughout the year, and you're likely to find a Lola front and center!

WHERE TO SPOT A LOLA: *The Philippines*

HOW TO GREET HER: *Take her hand and touch it to your forehead saying "Kumusta po"*

LOLA WISDOM: *Whatever you do, think about it seven times first*

Bon dia, Wela!

(weh-lah)

Aruba's slogan is "One Happy Island," and it is a place filled with music and dance. Aruban grandmas, called Welas, are also known for their joy and liveliness. Carnival is one of the most important dates in Aruba and a Wela might get involved by dancing, making costumes, or even playing in a band!

For most Welas, making sure their grandchildren are kind and well mannered is super important. A Wela can teach you Aruban manners, such as always making eye contact and using an open palm to show things instead of pointing your finger. Or she might help you learn polite phrases like please (por fabor) and thank you (danki) in Papiamento, the language most Arubans speak.

WHERE TO SPOT A WELA: *Aruba*

HOW TO GREET HER: *With a warm "Bon dia!"*

WELA WISDOM: *If you are too busy to laugh, you are too busy*

Hallo, Oma!

(oh-mah)

If you're looking for thrills and adventure, a Dutch grandma, or Oma, may be the perfect companion. You could join an Oma for a bike ride—in the Netherlands, there are more bicycles than there are people! And many Omas ride on special bikes called "Omafiets." Or an Oma might teach you how to ice-skate—another very popular Dutch pastime. Even breakfast would be fun with an Oma, as she'd probably treat you to some "hagelslag"—a famous Dutch dish made of bread, butter ... and sugary sprinkles. After all, you'll need lots of energy for all your adventures!

WHERE TO SPOT AN OMA: *The Netherlands*

HOW TO GREET HER: *Say "Hallo" and then give her three kisses on alternate cheeks*

OMA WISDOM: *Act normal, as that's crazy enough*

USEFUL PHRASE: *"Langzamer, oma!'" (Slow down, grandma!)*

Ni hǎo, Lǎolao / Nǎinai!

(lau-lo / ni-ni)

In Mandarin Chinese, a grandma has two names: a Lǎolao is your mom's mom, and a Nǎinai is your dad's mom. In China, it's very important to visit your grandparents regularly—in fact it's against the law if you don't! It's called the Elderly Rights Law, and it's all about making sure older people are taken care of. But Lǎolaos and Nǎinais make sure to reciprocate all that love and time! Many help take care of their grandchildren, and when babies are first born, a Lǎolao or Nǎinai often moves in to help out. This means the new mom gets some rest, while the grandma gets to spend time with and enjoy her new grandbaby!

WHERE TO SPOT A LĂOLAO / NĂINAI: China

HOW TO GREET HER: With a handshake and say, "Ni hǎo"

LĂOLAO / NĂINAI WISDOM: The one who asks is a fool for five minutes, but the one who doesn't ask remains a fool forever

Salam, Bibi-jan!

(bee-bee-jan)

When you're feeling kind of lost, you can always depend on a Bibi-jan. In Afghanistan, grandmas are very respected and families often turn to their Bibi-jan for help and advice. Many Bibi-jans live with their families—this way, they can share their wisdom and skills every day of the week!

One of these skills might be making a kite. Kite flying is hugely popular in Afghanistan and a creative Bibi-jan might help you make a beautiful design, then cheer you on as you fly it! Poetry is also treasured in Afghanistan, and a Bibi-jan might like to share with you some of her favorite poems or even teach you how to write a "Landay," which is a short form of Afghan poetry.

WHERE TO SPOT A BIBI-JAN: *Afghanistan*

HOW TO GREET HER: *Place your right hand over your heart and say, "Salam"*

BIBI-JAN WISDOM: *A river is made drop by drop*

WRITE A LANDAY FOR A GRANDMA

To write your own traditional Afghan poem, you just need to think of two lines. The first line should have nine syllables, and the second should have thirteen. It doesn't need to rhyme (unless you want it to!).

TOP LANDAY TIPS:

✭ Think of all the special things about the grandma you're writing for.

✭ Decide on the tone—do you want it to be funny, sweet, or something else?

✭ Make a note of your favorite words.

✭ A Landay is short, so decide from your notes what you think this grandma would most like you to say.

✭ Start putting it together—if the syllables aren't right, go back to your list of favorite words to see if any of those make a better fit.

✭ When you're happy, give or read it to your grandma of choice, accompanied by a hug!

No matter where in the world she's from, or whether she's near or far, a grandma is someone to lean on, to learn from, and to love!

Thank you to your grandma, and to all grandmas, everywhere.

Thank you for ...

Telling us
secrets

Making us
laugh

Soothing
remedies

Sharing
advice

Being our
friend

Family
traditions

Being proud
of us

Paying
attention

Helping us
grow

Setting an
example

Giving us
treats

Keeping us
warm

Precious
memories

For Nora, Nancy, and all the Mamgus. x — D. A. B.
To my dear grandmas, Esther and Bea, with love. — A. L.

Brimming with creative inspiration, how-to projects, and useful information to enrich your everyday life, Quarto Knows is a favorite destination for those pursuing their interests and passions. Visit our site and dig deeper with our books into your area of interest: Quarto Creates, Quarto Cooks, Quarto Homes, Quarto Lives, Quarto Drives, Quarto Explores, Quarto Gifts, or Quarto Kids.

First published in 2021 by Wide Eyed Editions, an imprint of The Quarto Group.
100 Cummings Center, Suite 265D, Beverly, MA 01915 USA.
T +1 978-282-9590 F +1 978-283-2742 www.QuartoKnows.com

ISBN 978-0-7112-6108-2

The illustrations were created digitally
Set in Recoleta and Neutraface

Published by Georgia Amson-Bradshaw
Designed by Kate Haynes
Edited by Hannah Dove
Production by Dawn Cameron

Manufactured in Guangdong, China TT062021

9 8 7 6 5 4 3 2 1

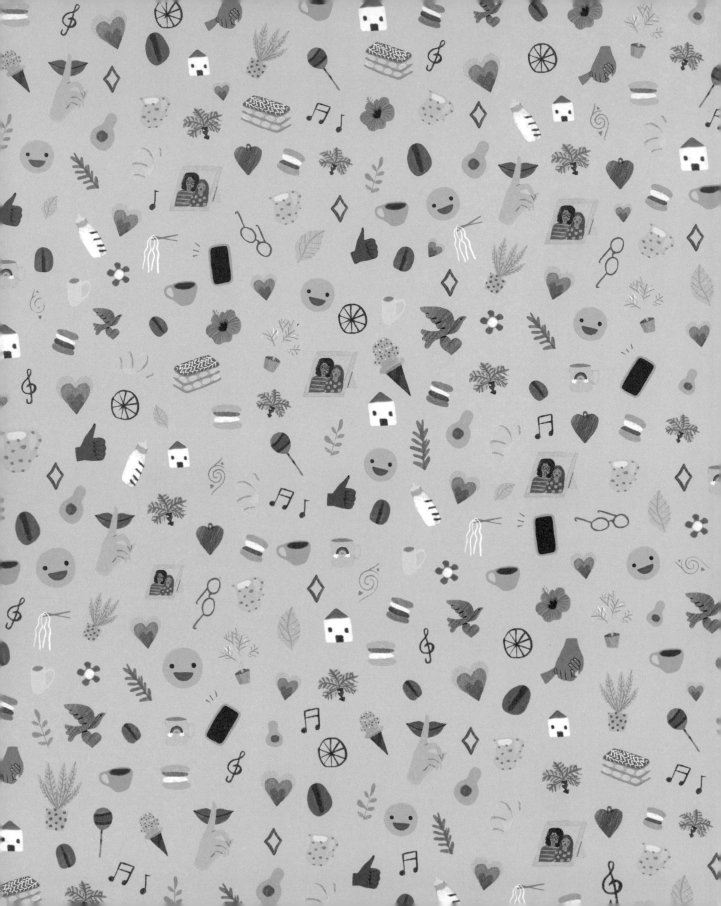